Gift To A Friend

written and illustrated by
Barb Suvanto and Cheryl McCarten

TooPicky Press
Hudson, Wisconsin

Published by:
TooPicky Press
1513 Ward Avenue
Hudson, WI 54016

Printed by:
Worzalla
P.O. Box 307
Stevens Point, WI 54481-0307

Design and layout by:
Mark Carey

Copyright ©2003 Barb Suvanto and Cheryl McCarten

All rights reserved. No part of this publication may be reproduced in any form without the prior written permission of the publisher.

ISBN: 0-9729431-0-2

Published in the United States of America

"Friendship is the golden ribbon that ties the world together."
- Author Unknown

This book is dedicated to the friends who inspired us to write it...
Nixola Pierce, Pam Templeton and Robin Rose

We also dedicate this work to our families who are
the inspiration for the rest of life...
Miikka, Jenny,
Brian, Kelly, Daniel and Sarah

Special thanks go to the following people:

Thomas O'Connell
Jill Tammen-Higgins
Cindy Brown
Micki Thompson
Connie Simpson
Bobbie O'Connell
Tammy O'Connell
Robin Waldroff
Sandy Trainor
Bettie Peterson
Studio 94 Hair Design Staff

The twilight softly comes to life
with the first winter's snow,

Gentle, white and glistening
by the moonlight set aglow.

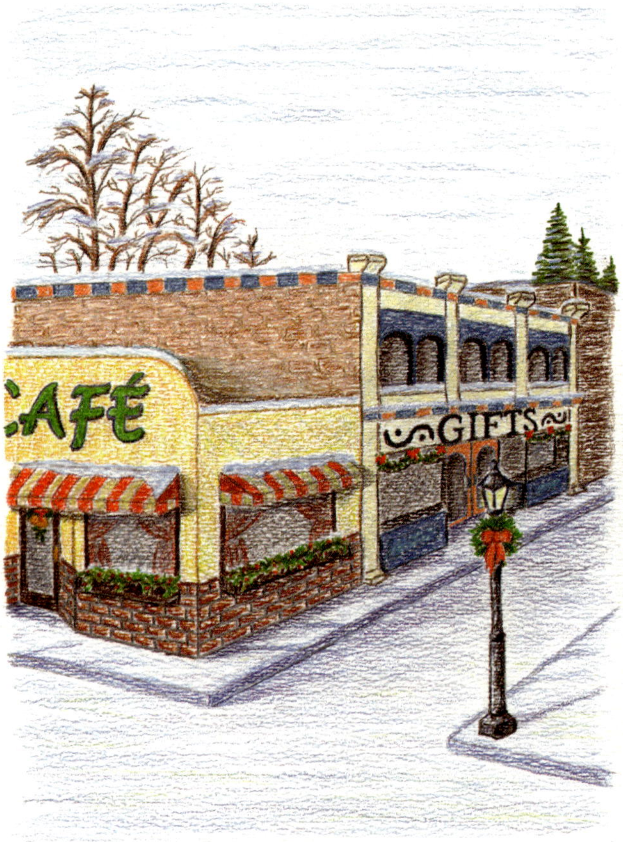
CAFÉ
GIFTS

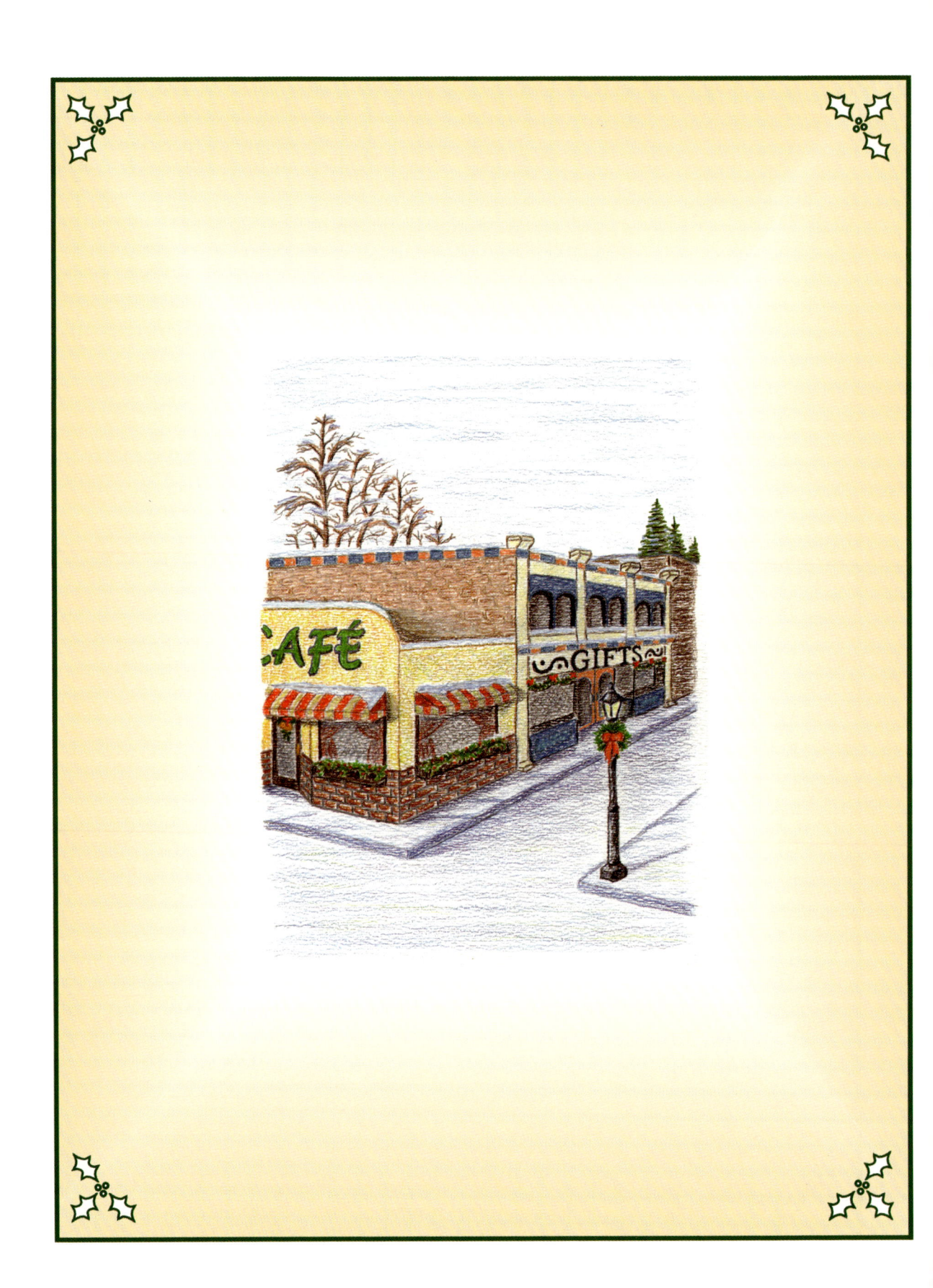

High spirits now commencing in
the small towns far and near,

The holidays approaching – yes,
it is that time of year.

Shop windows gaily dressed in their
seasonal red and green,

Fresh mistletoe and holly hang,
delighted to be seen.

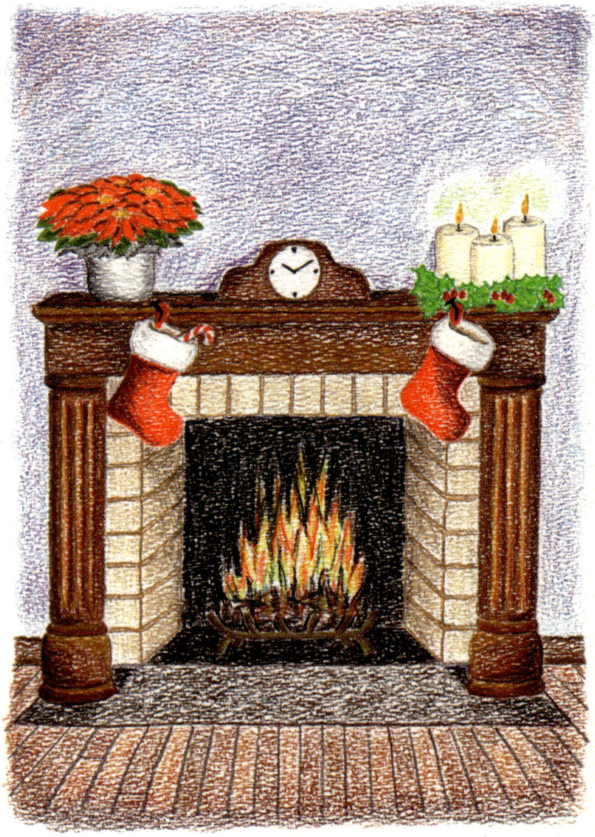

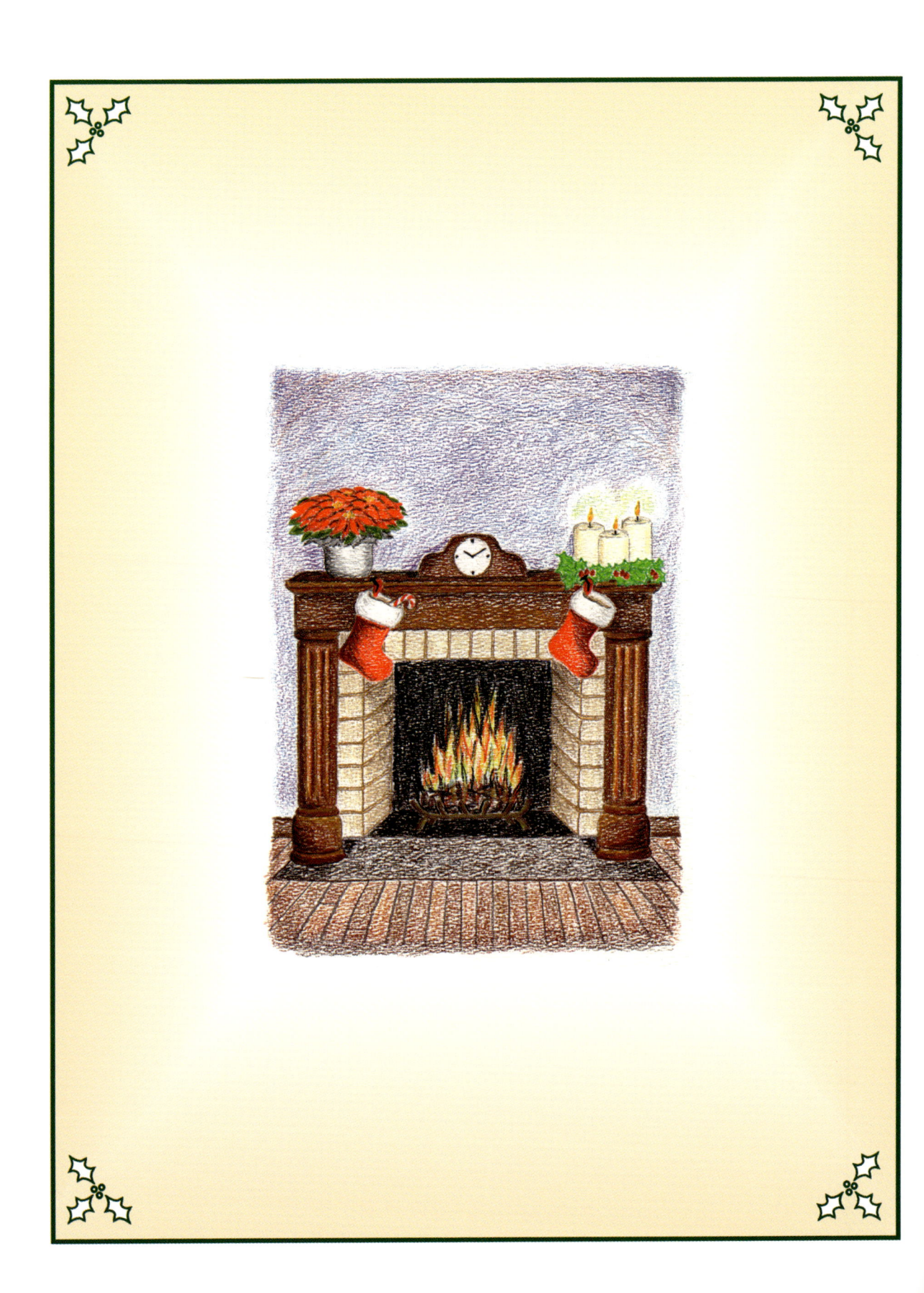

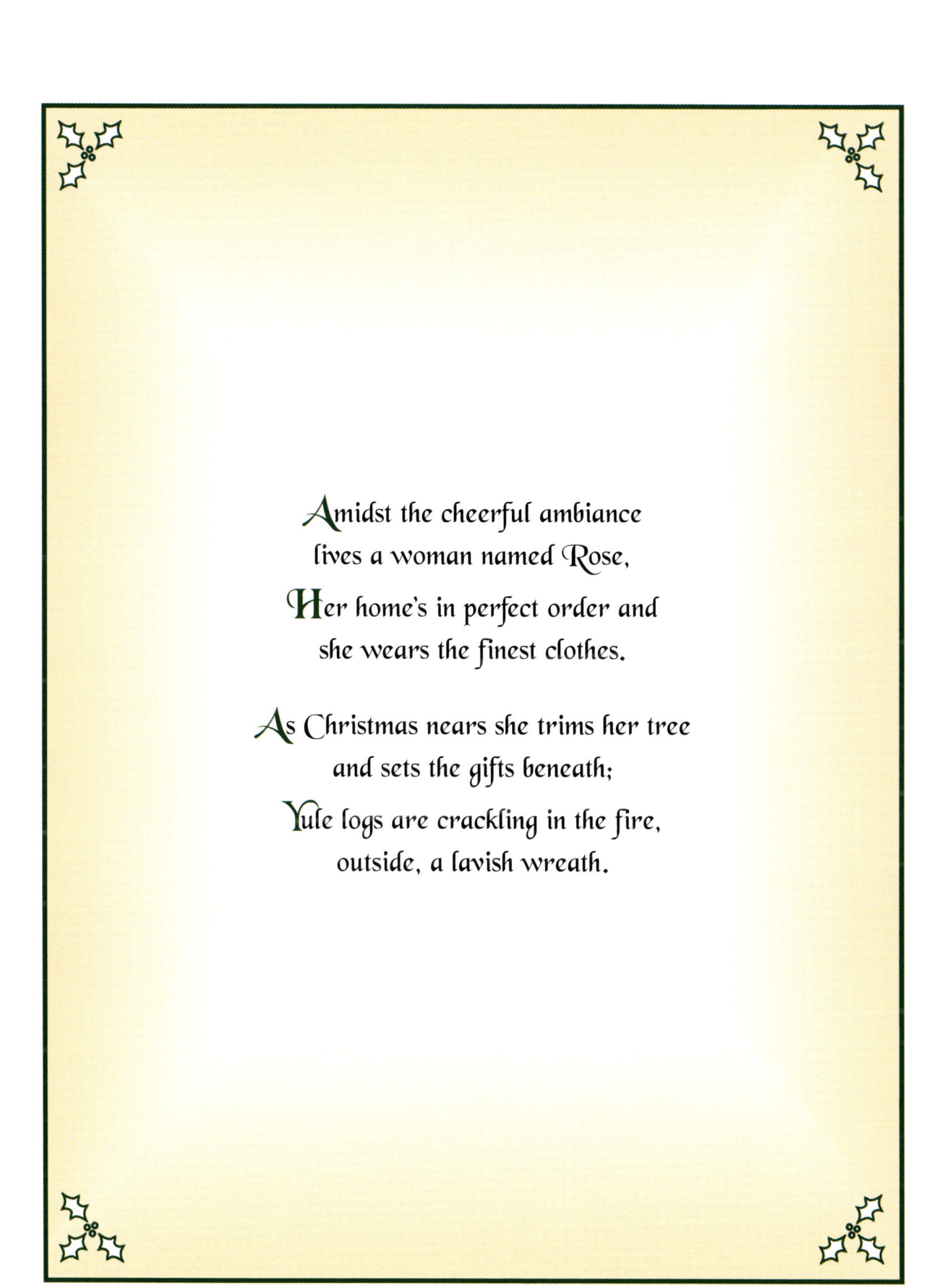

Amidst the cheerful ambiance
lives a woman named Rose,
Her home's in perfect order and
she wears the finest clothes.

As Christmas nears she trims her tree
and sets the gifts beneath;
Yule logs are crackling in the fire,
outside, a lavish wreath.

Rose is further on than most
concerning the festive race,
With only one left on her list –
her dearest friend named Grace.

Rose and Grace met years ago, but
if asked exactly when,
Neither one could tell for sure
the number of years it's been.

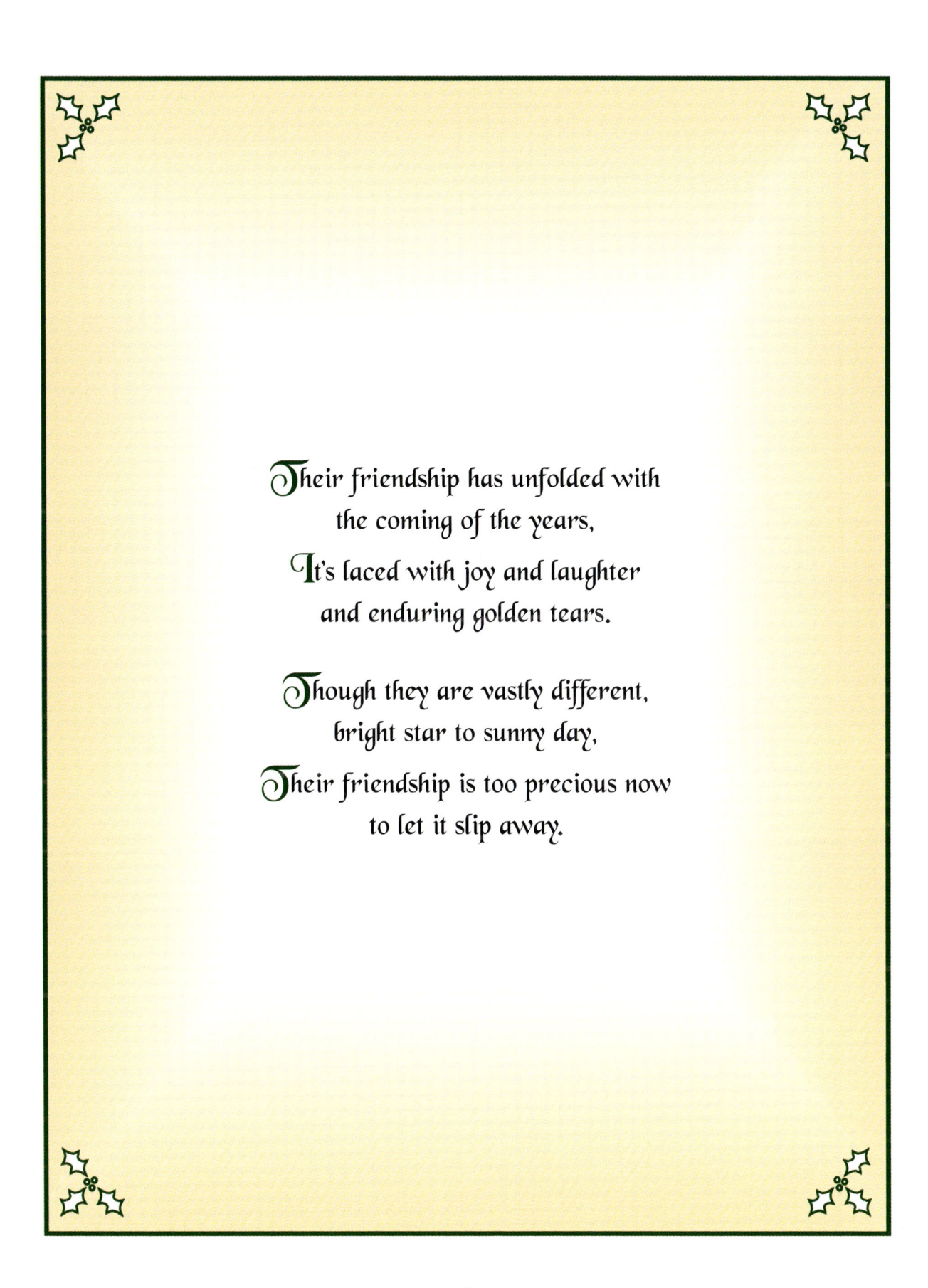

Their friendship has unfolded with
the coming of the years,
It's laced with joy and laughter
and enduring golden tears.

Though they are vastly different,
bright star to sunny day,
Their friendship is too precious now
to let it slip away.

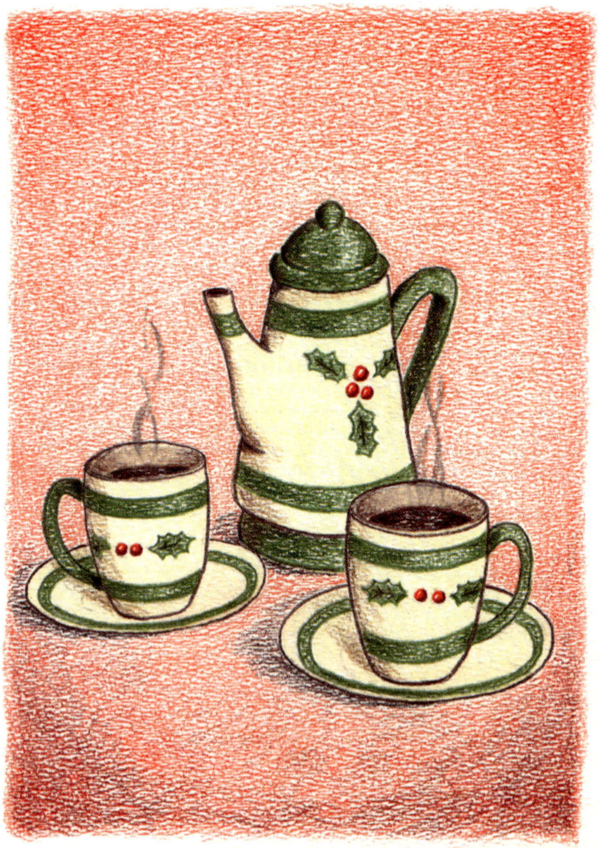

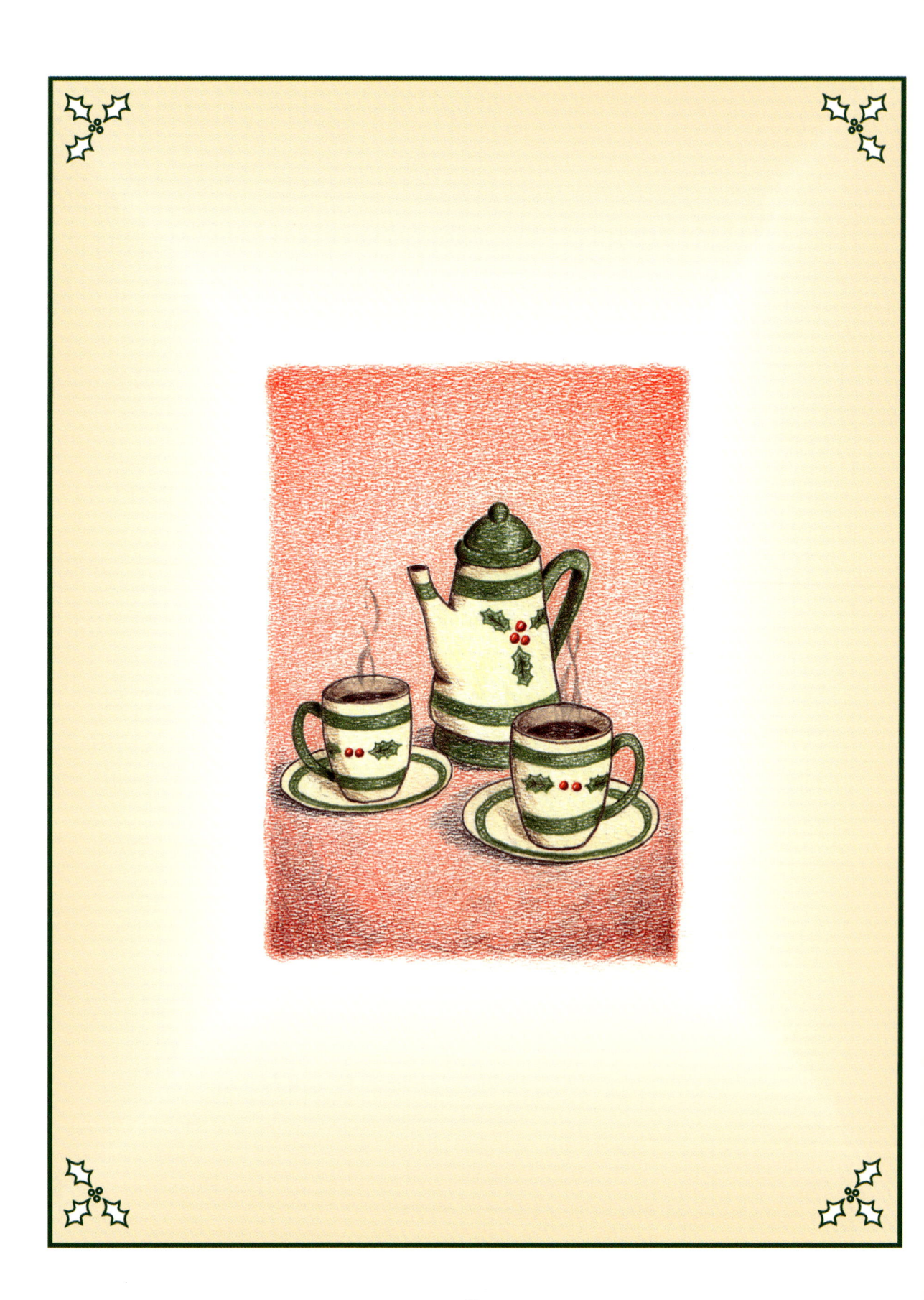

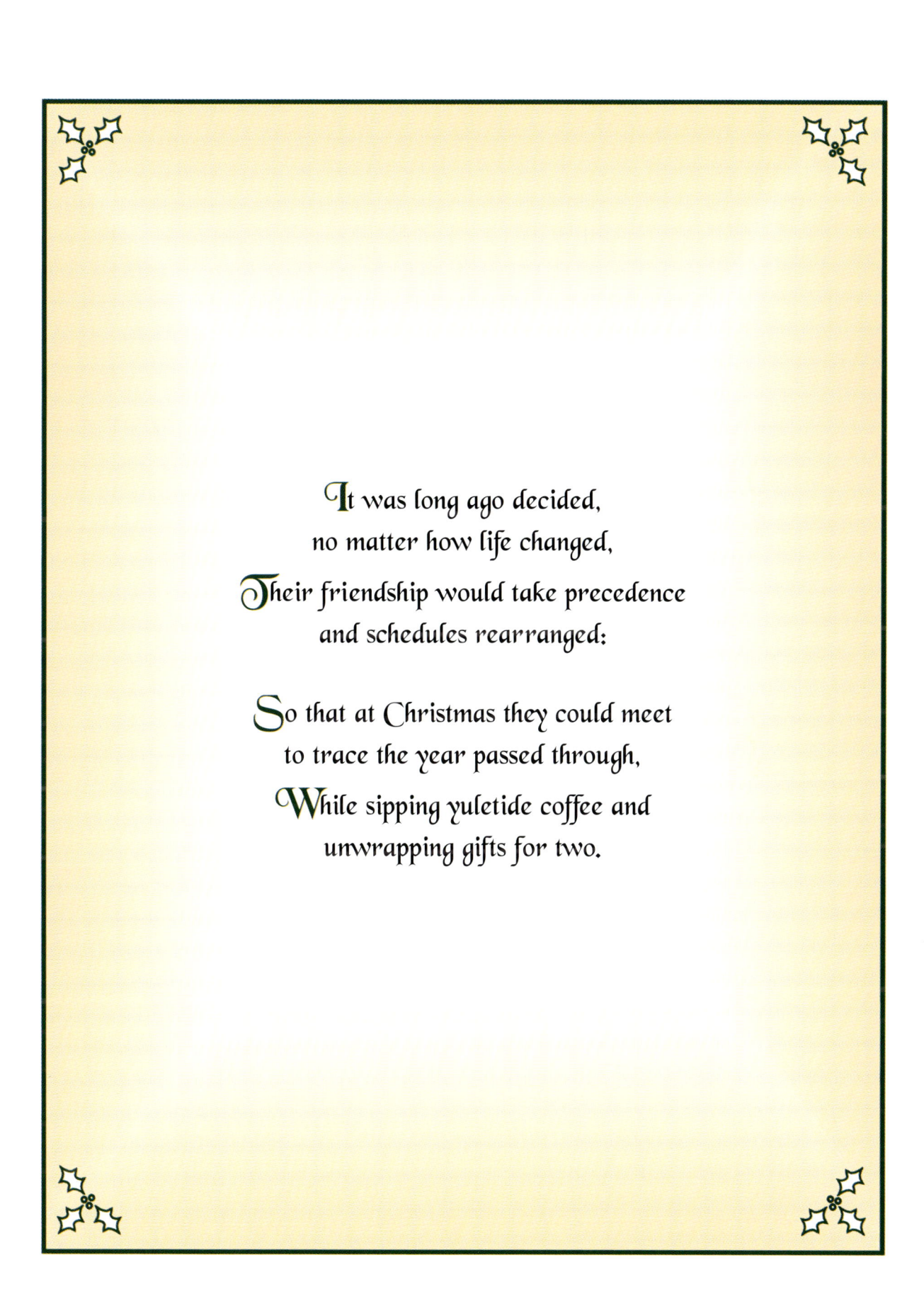

It was long ago decided,
no matter how life changed,
Their friendship would take precedence
and schedules rearranged:

So that at Christmas they could meet
to trace the year passed through,
While sipping yuletide coffee and
unwrapping gifts for two.

DECEMBER
S M T W T F S
1 2 3 4 5 6
7 8 9 10 11 12 13
14 15 16 17 18 19 20
21 22 23 24 25 26 27
28 29 30 31

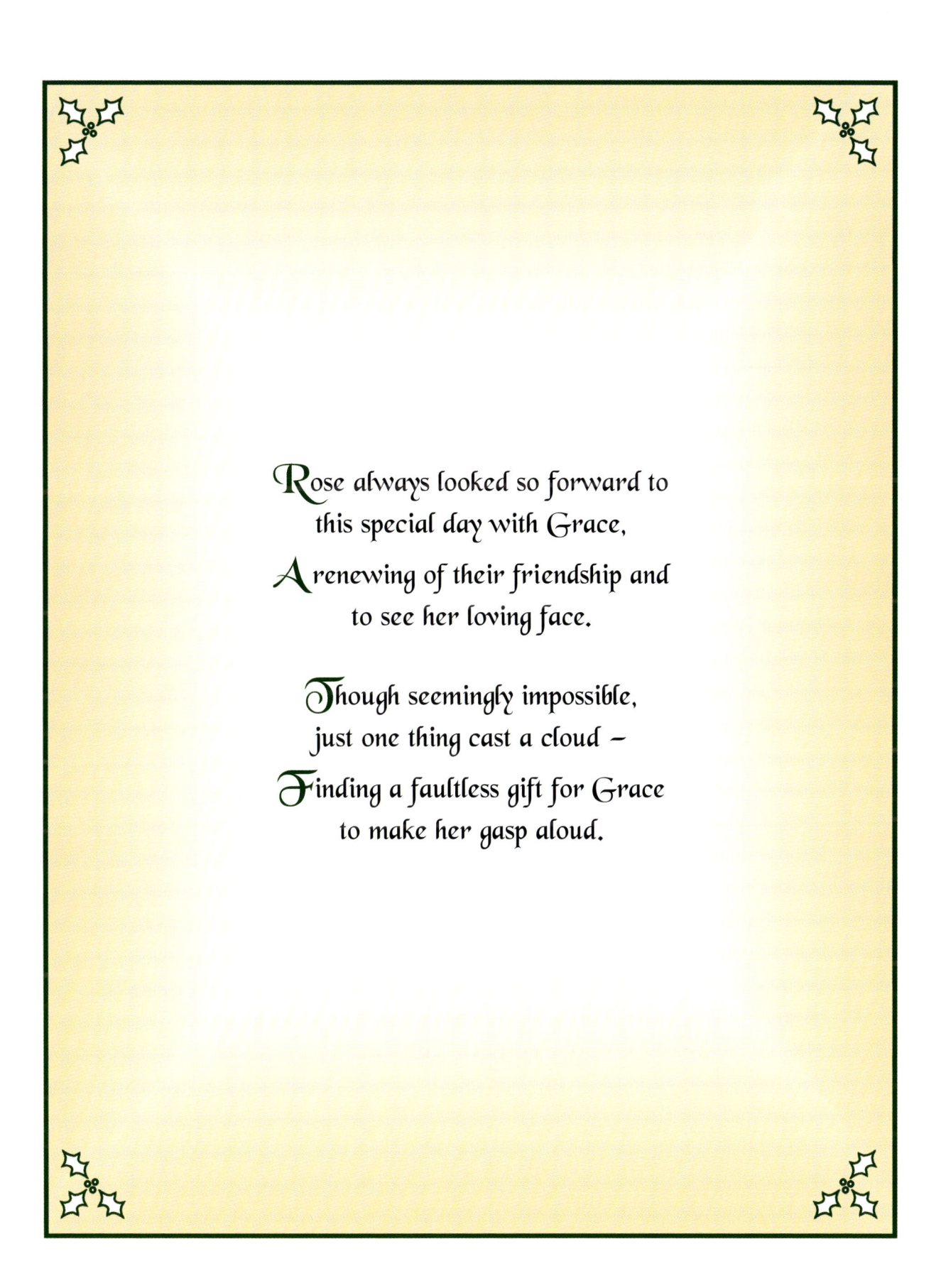

Rose always looked so forward to
this special day with Grace,
A renewing of their friendship and
to see her loving face.

Though seemingly impossible,
just one thing cast a cloud –
Finding a faultless gift for Grace
to make her gasp aloud.

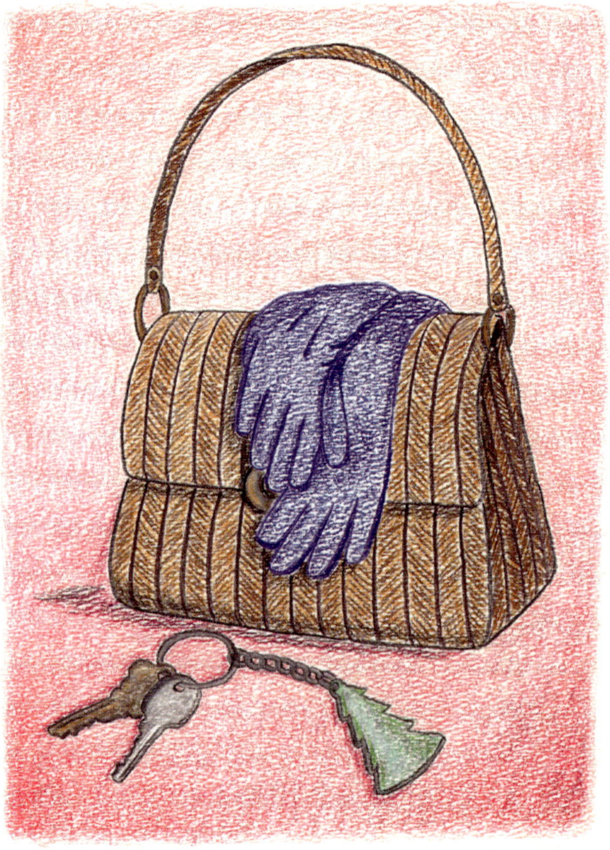

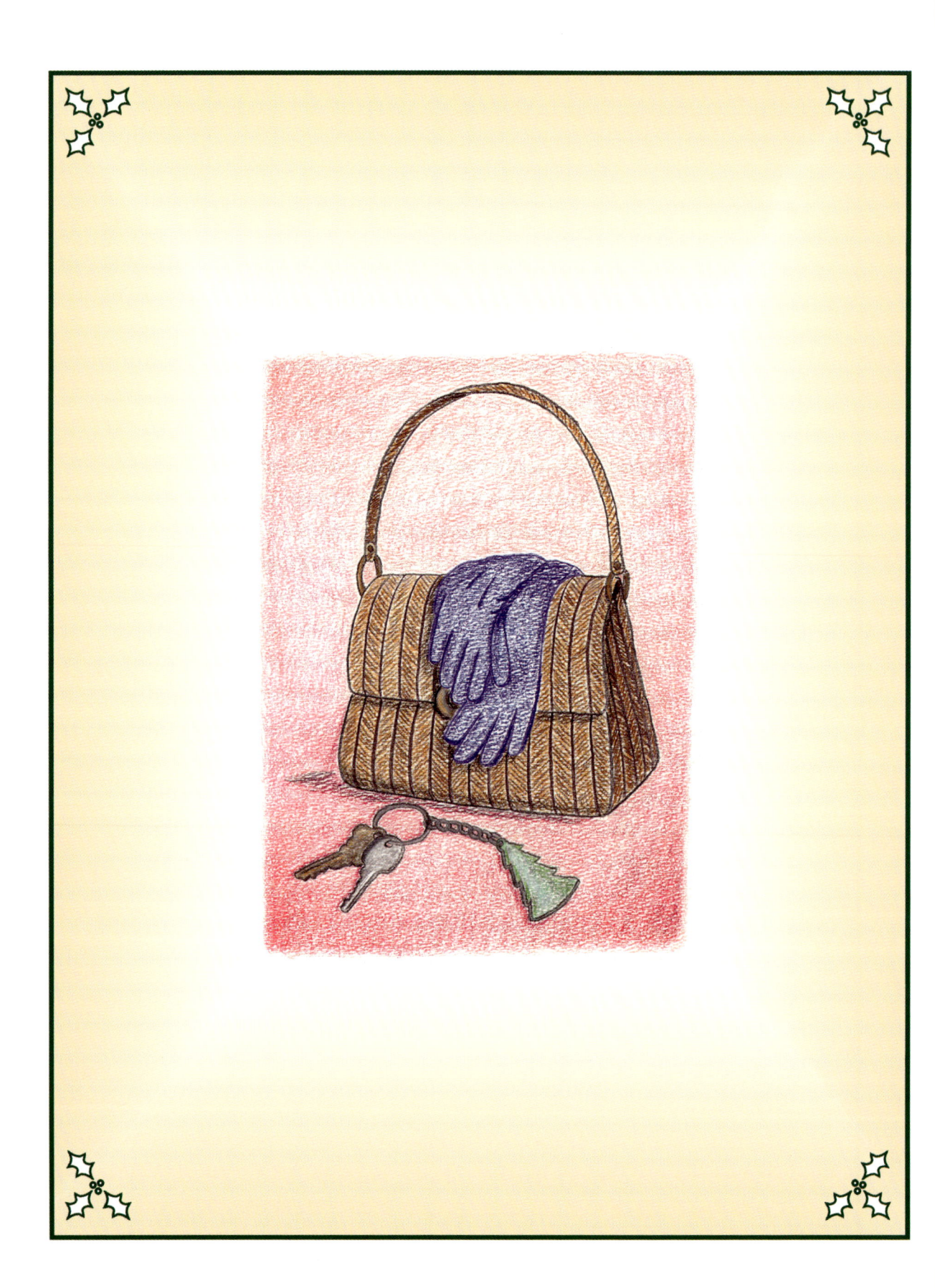

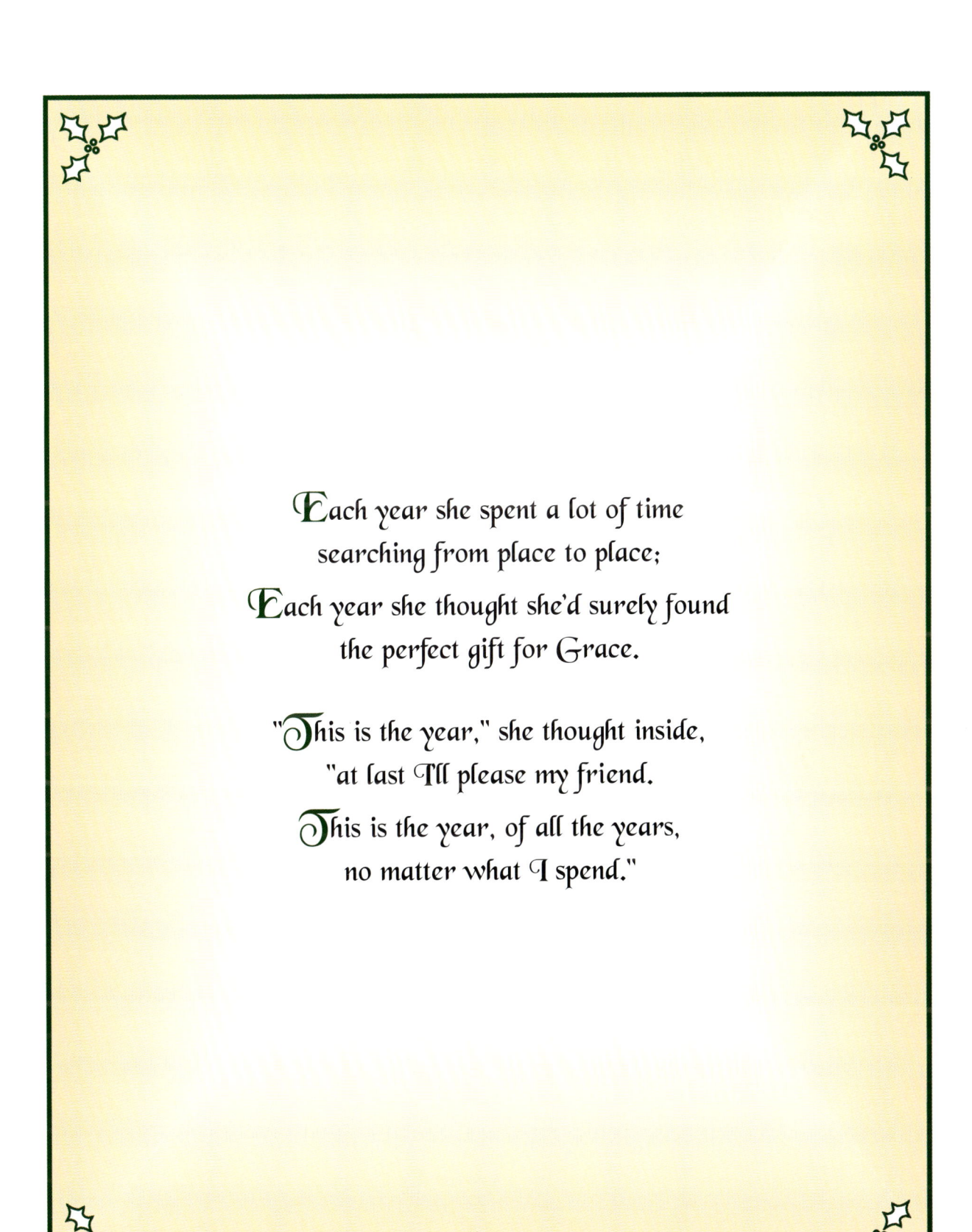

Each year she spent a lot of time
searching from place to place;
Each year she thought she'd surely found
the perfect gift for Grace.

"This is the year," she thought inside,
"at last I'll please my friend.
This is the year, of all the years,
no matter what I spend."

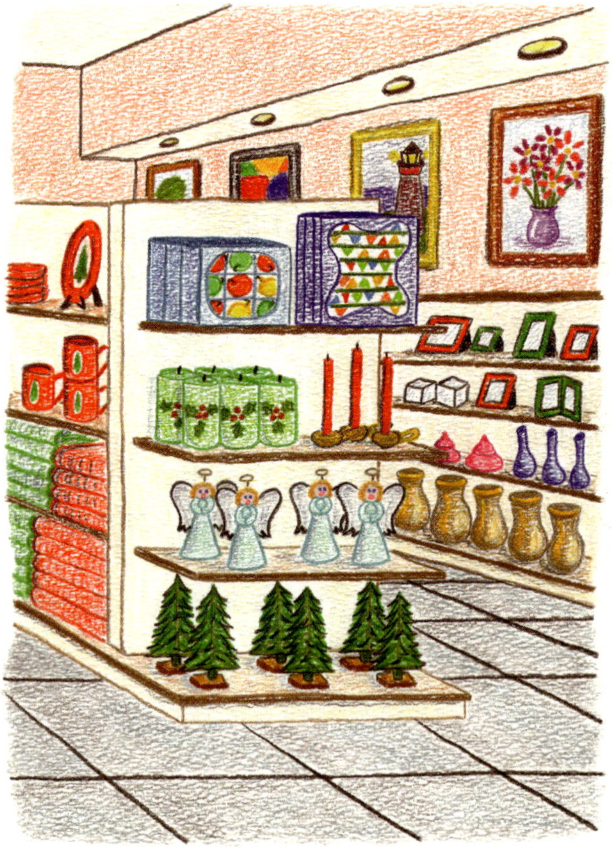

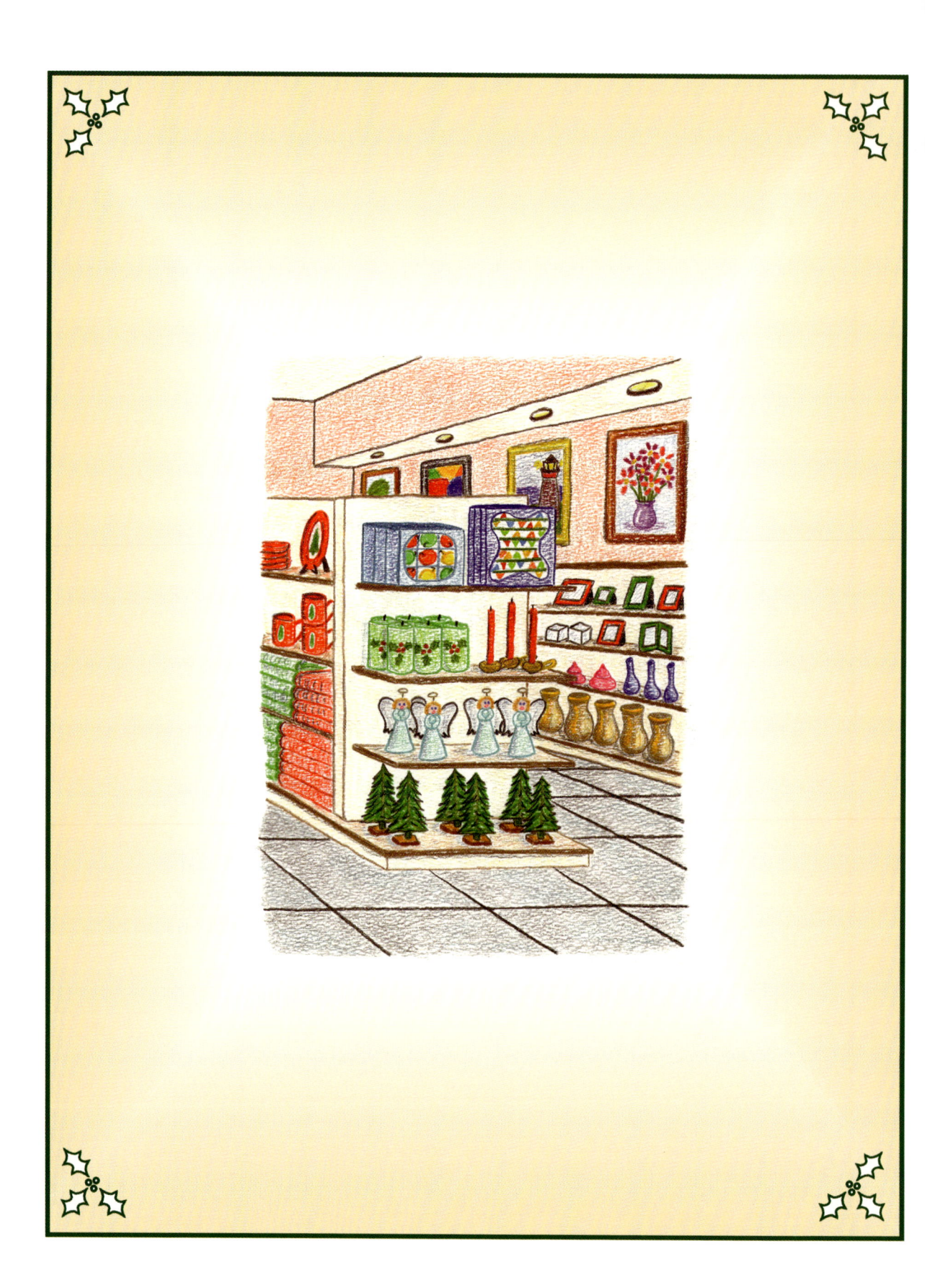

She stepped into a gift shop and
went up and down each aisle;
All of a sudden, there it was –
the gift that made Rose smile!

She carefully wrapped the trinket,
tied on a pretty bow,
For Grace to open and exclaim,
"Perfect! How did you know?"

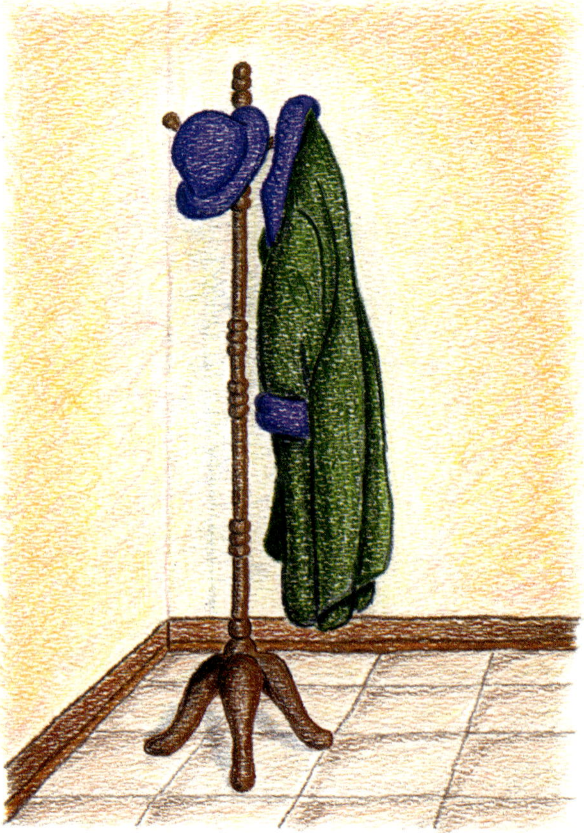

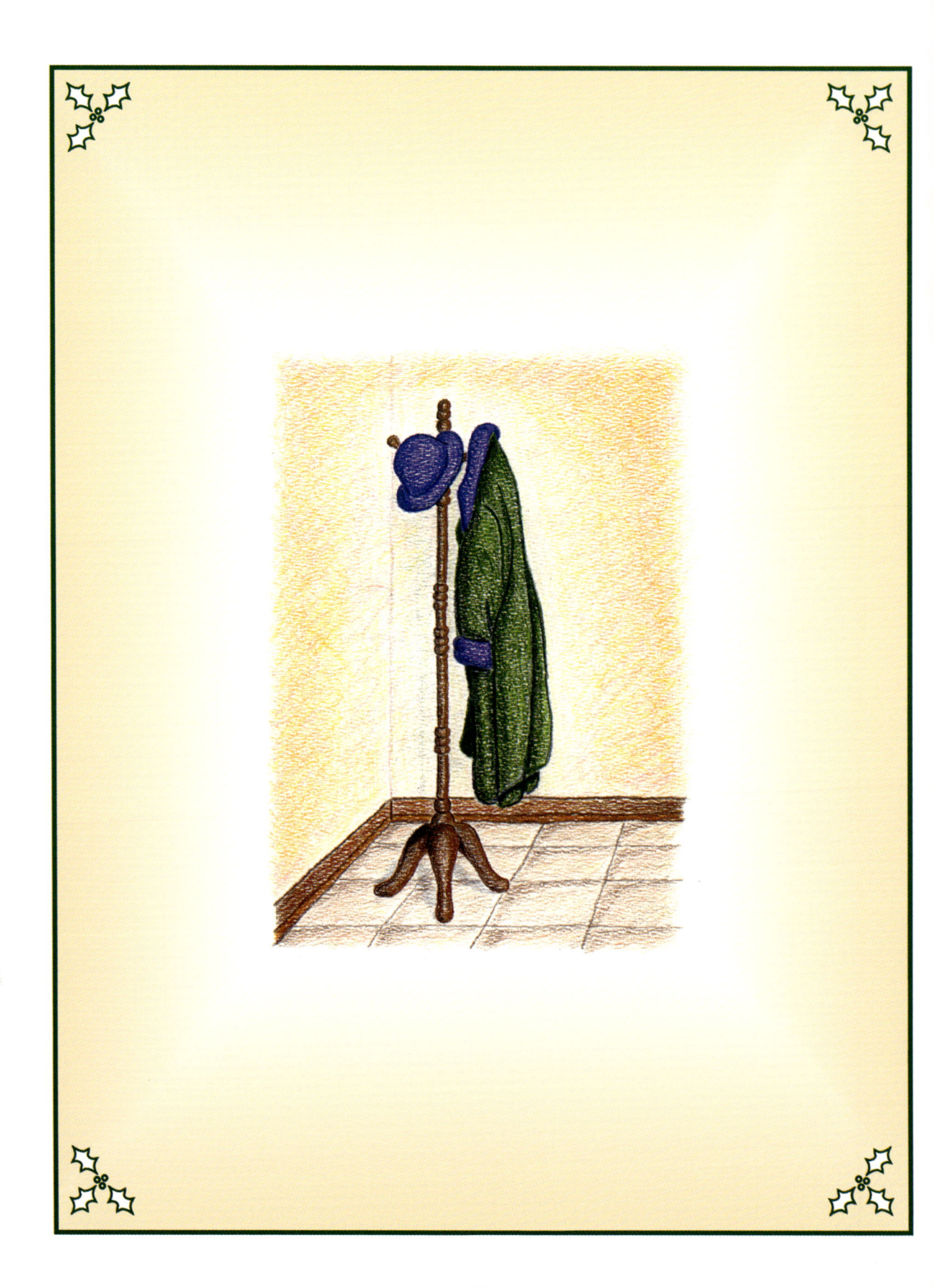

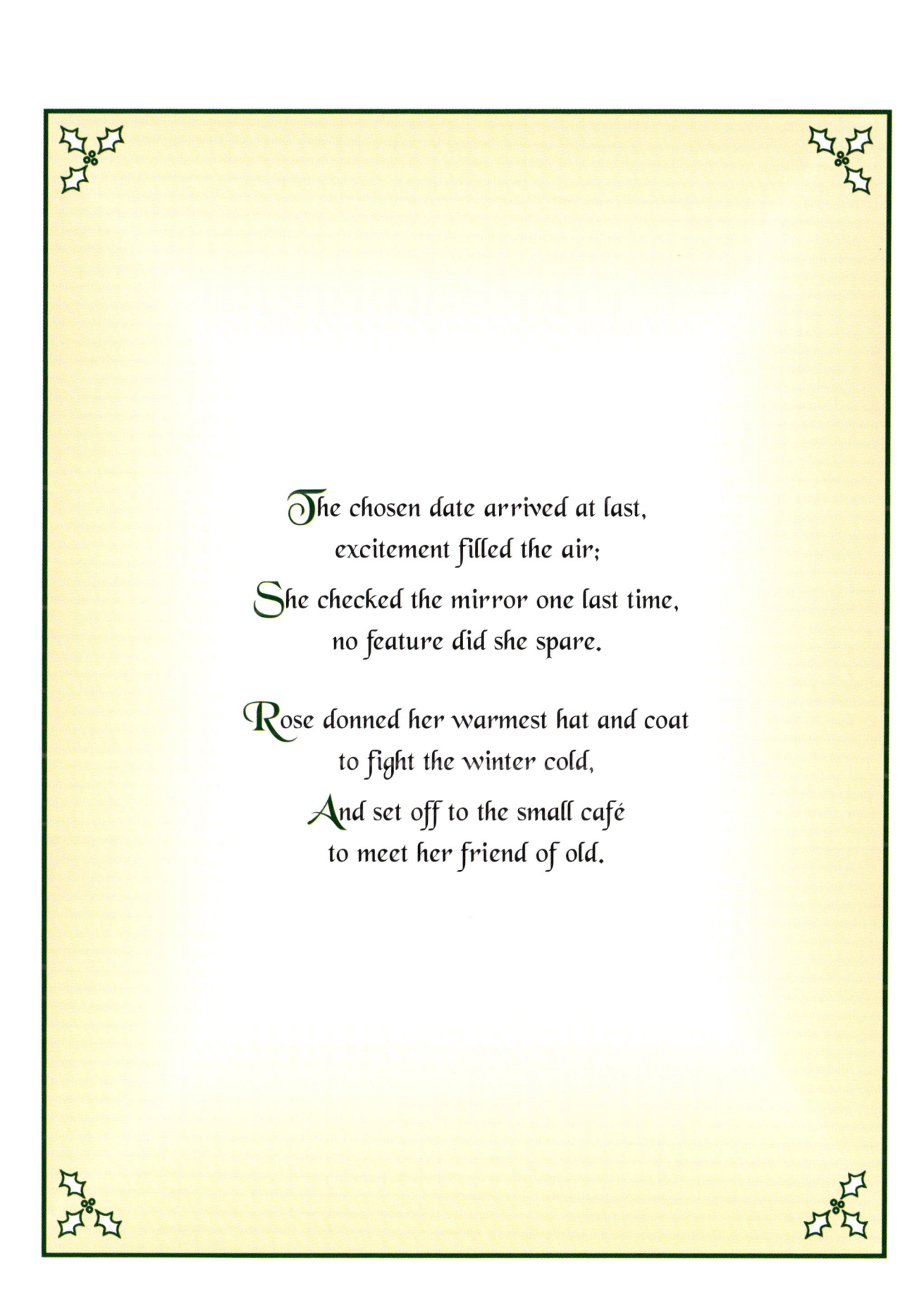

The chosen date arrived at last,
excitement filled the air;
She checked the mirror one last time,
no feature did she spare.

Rose donned her warmest hat and coat
to fight the winter cold,
And set off to the small café
to meet her friend of old.

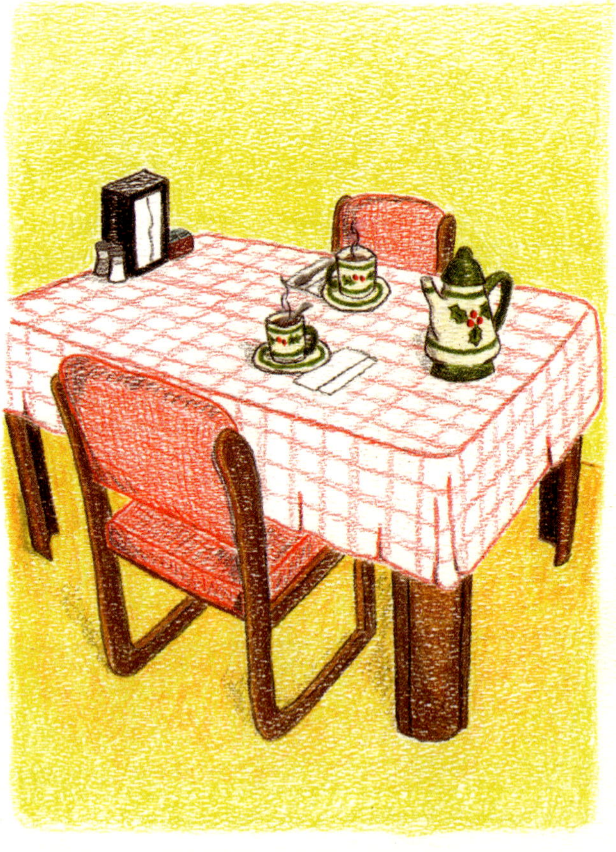

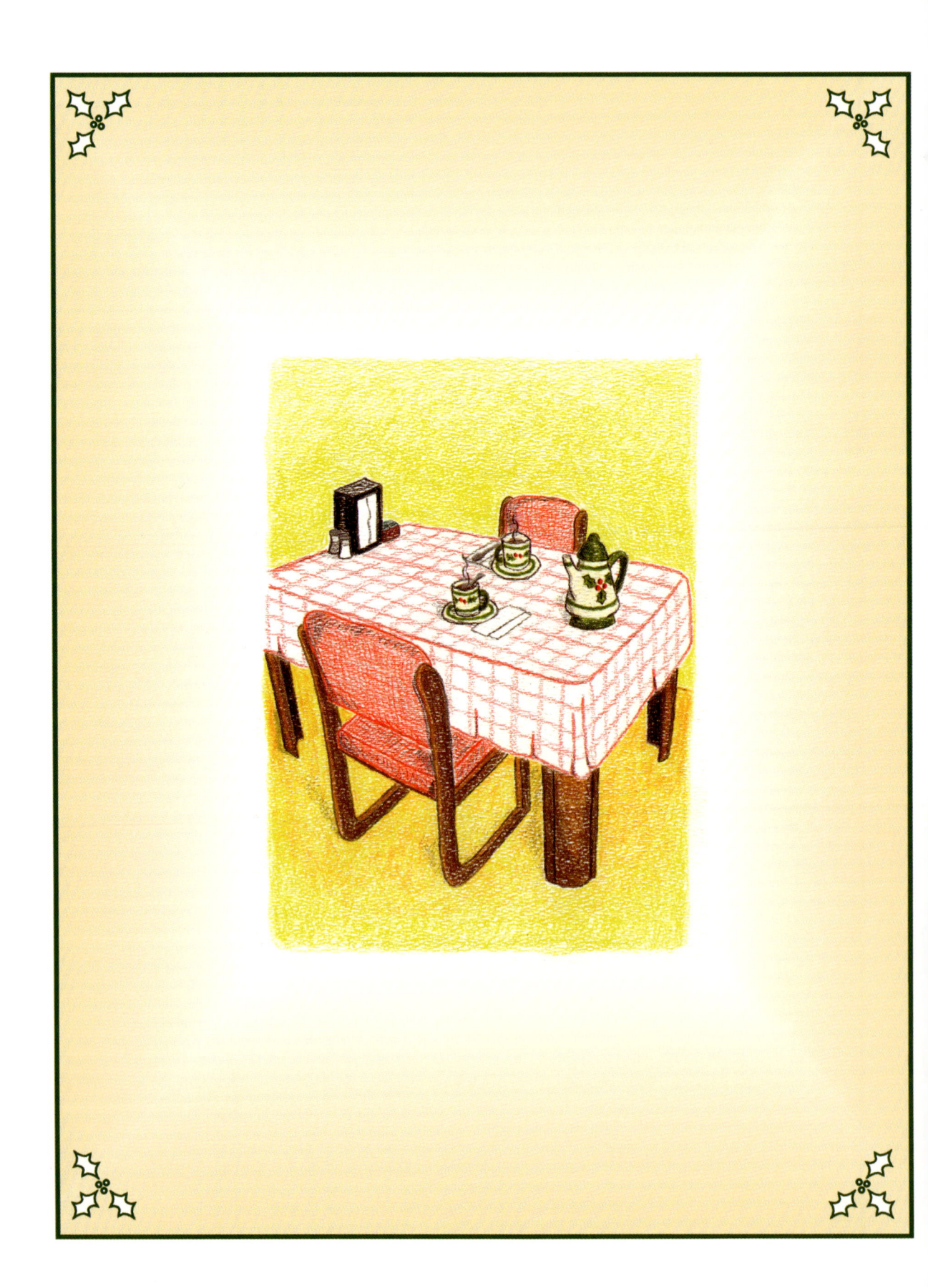

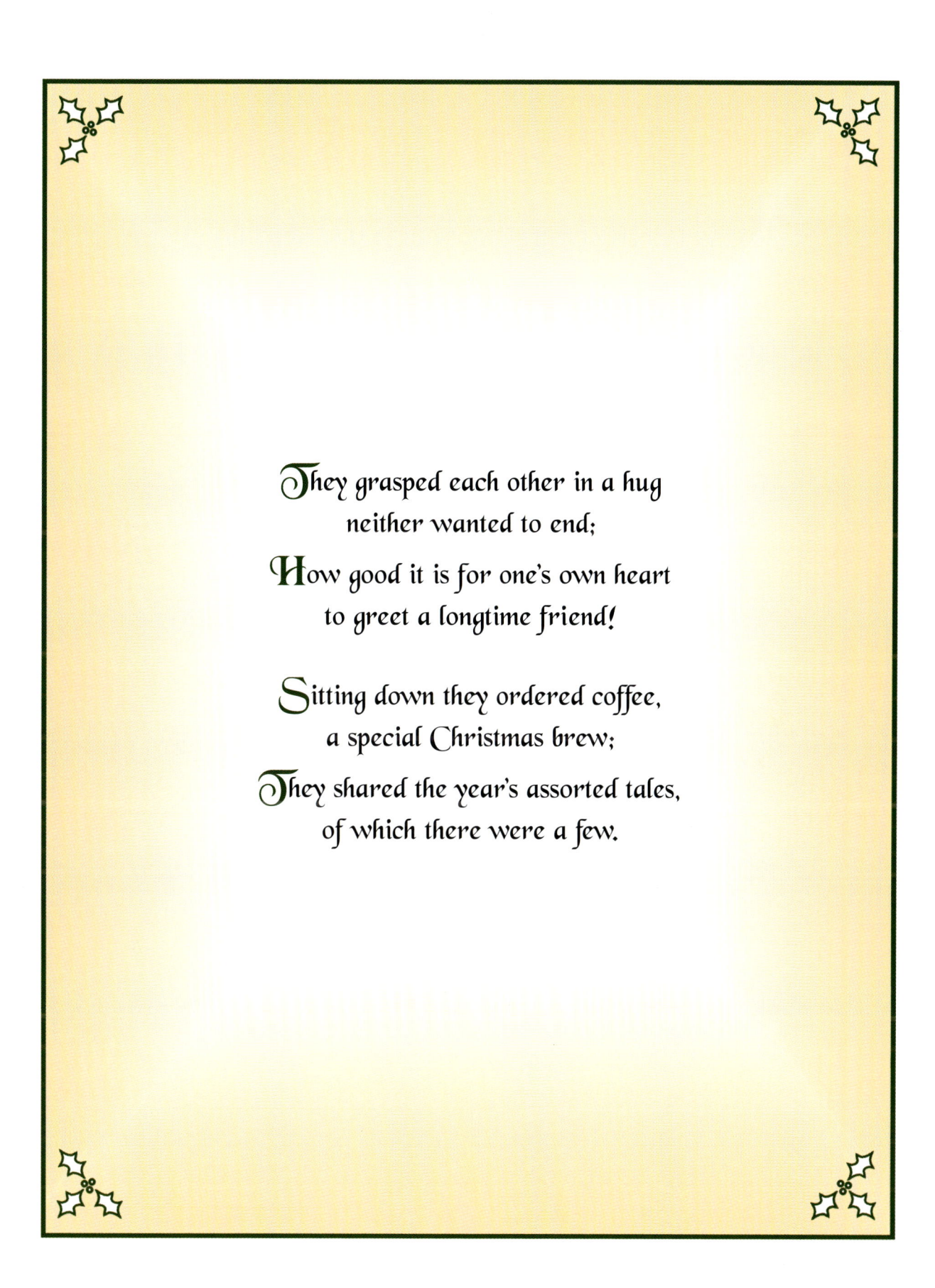

They grasped each other in a hug
neither wanted to end;
How good it is for one's own heart
to greet a longtime friend!

Sitting down they ordered coffee,
a special Christmas brew;
They shared the year's assorted tales,
of which there were a few.

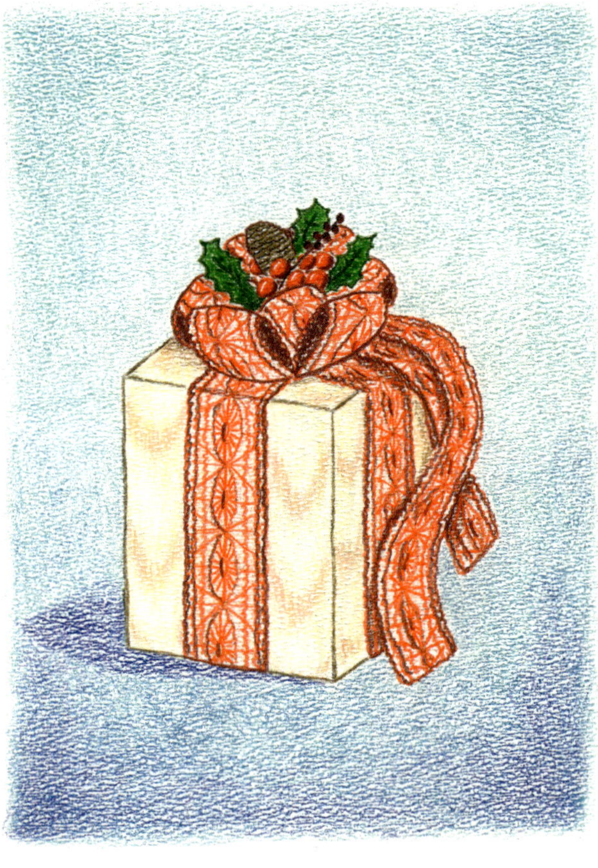

The hours flew by so quickly
and late afternoon drew near;
Eagerly, Rose said to Grace,
"It's time for gifts, my dear."

Rose went first, a bit excited
to give her gift to Grace,
Wrapped up in satin paper with
a bow made out of lace.

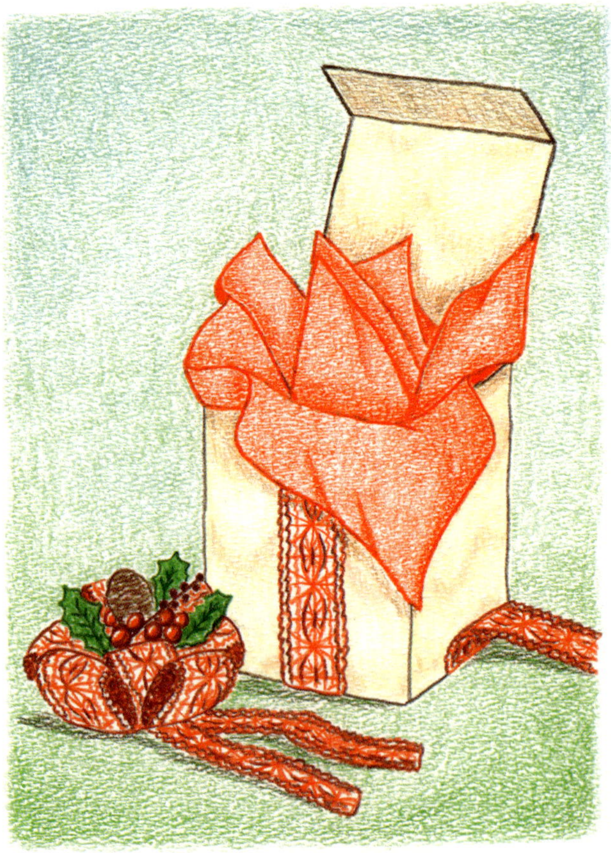

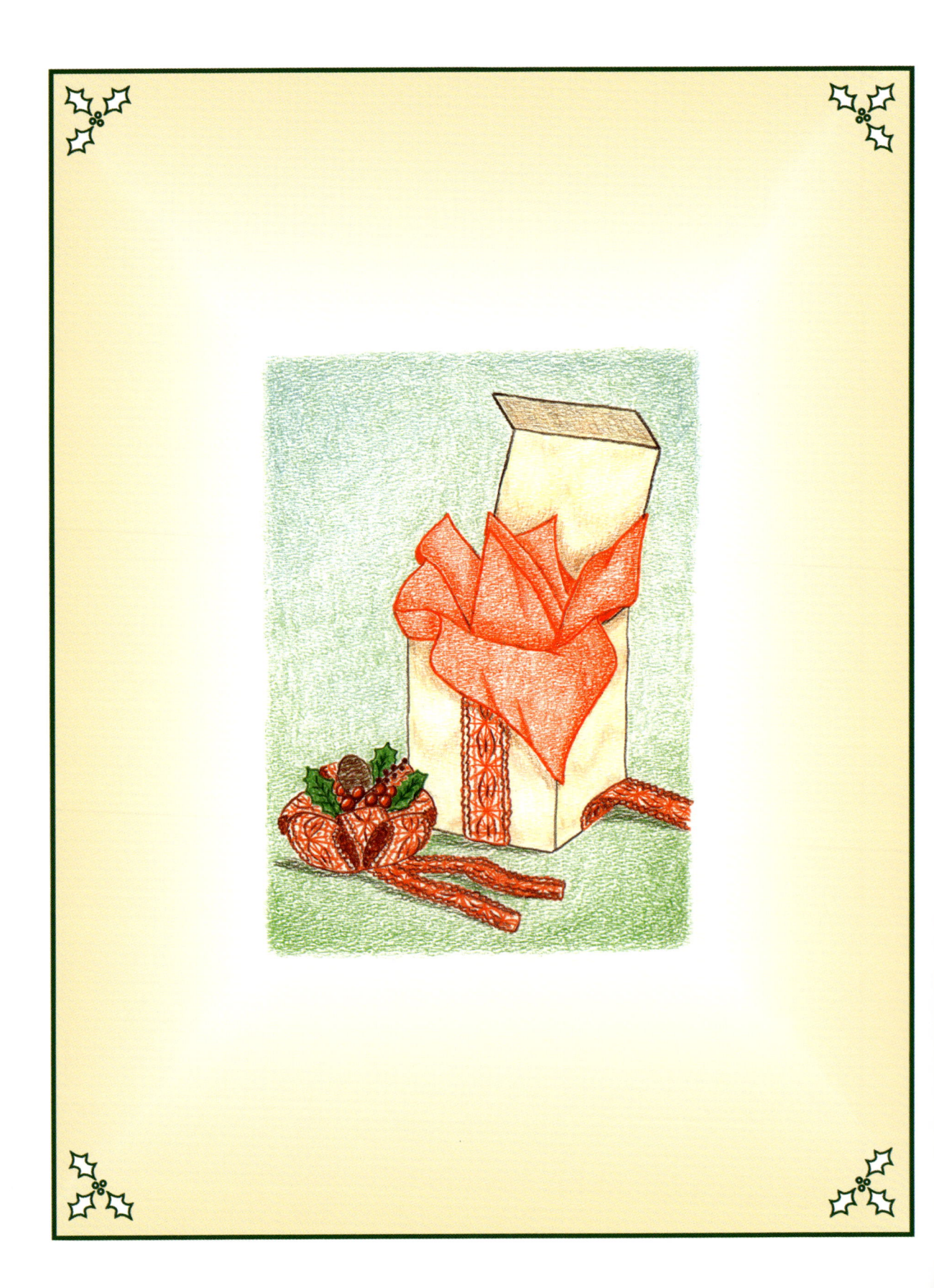

Rose watched her as she opened it,
becoming very shy;
Grace took the trinket from its box
exclaiming, "My, oh my!"

Indeed, this was the year at last
Rose saw her pure delight,
But Grace then set her gift aside
as if it seemed too trite.

Though Grace was more than gracious as
she said her thanks with tact,
Rose, in her heart began to see
there's something her gift lacked.

Averse to dampen spirits, yet,
just one thing she must know –
How her gifts had missed the mark
since so long a time ago.

"Oh, Grace, please tell me why it is
you set my gift aside?
Is something wrong with what I chose?"
Rose sniffed and nearly cried.

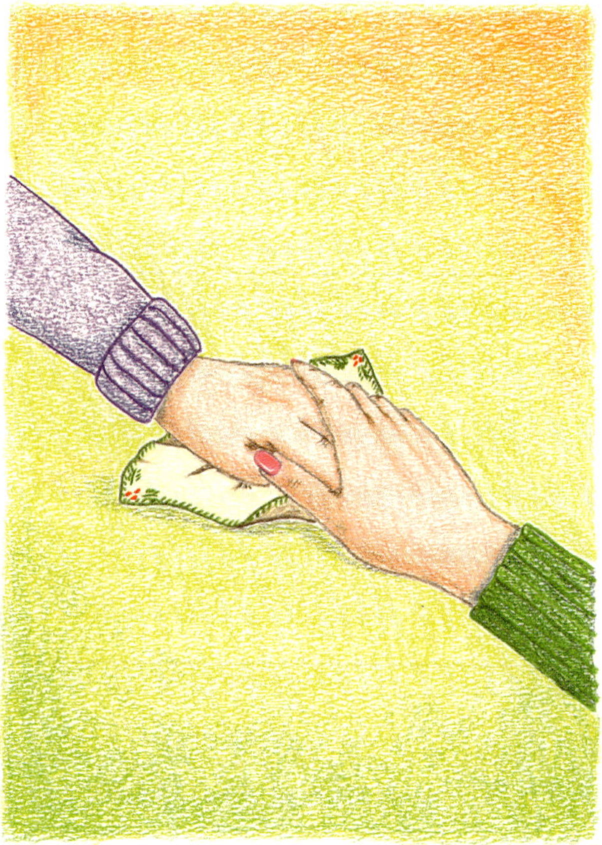

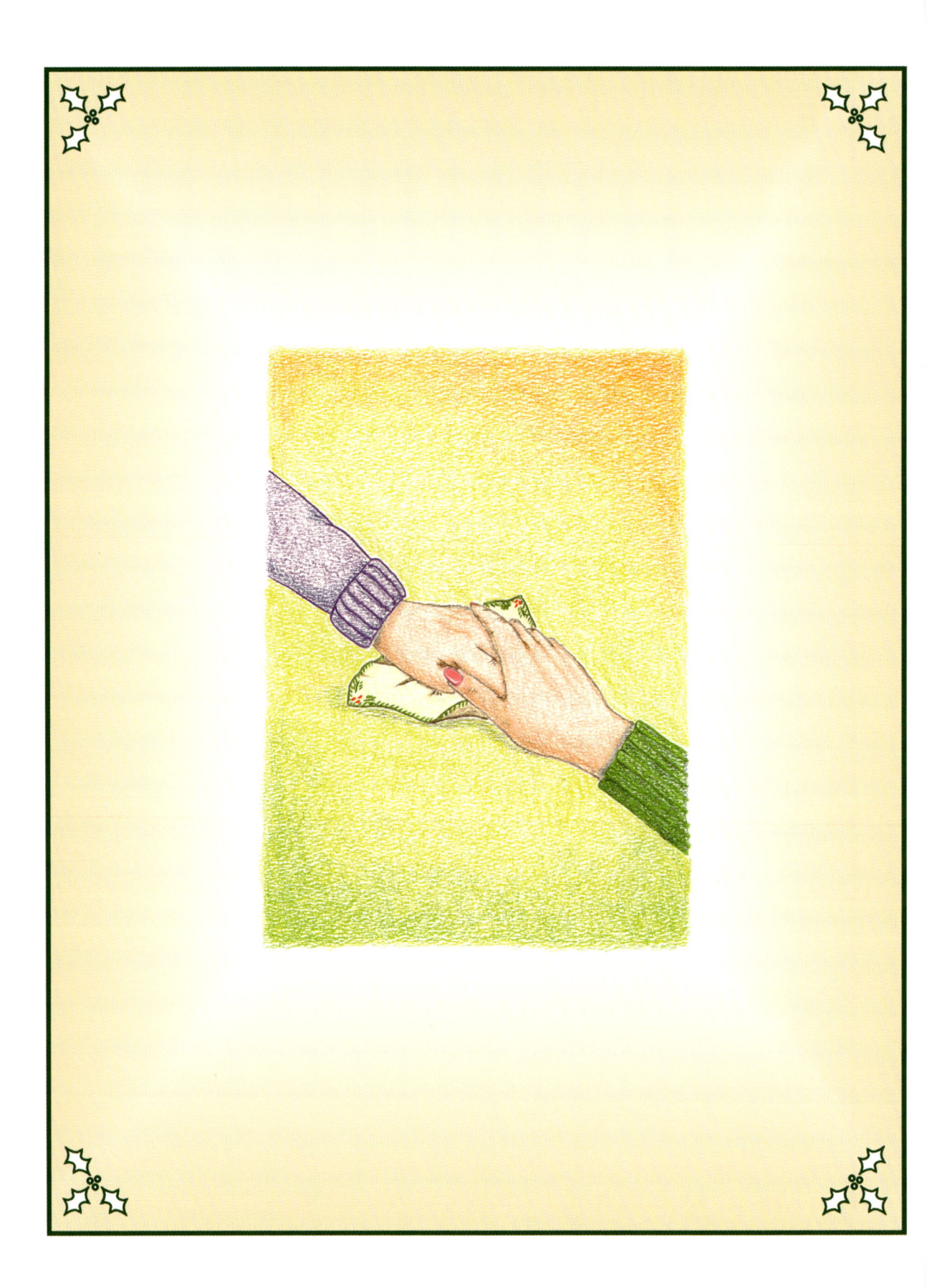

"Together we have met here
in this café all these years;
I've seen you open all your gifts
and little joy appears."

Grace covered Rose's hand to hold it
gently in her own;
She looked in her friend's troubled eyes
where seeds of doubt were sown.

"Oh, Rose, you wonderful, dear fool!
My joy is not complete?
My cherished friend for all these years,
in this there's no deceit:

"I love the things you've given me,
each and every one;
This Christmas coffee meeting
is so treasured when it's done!

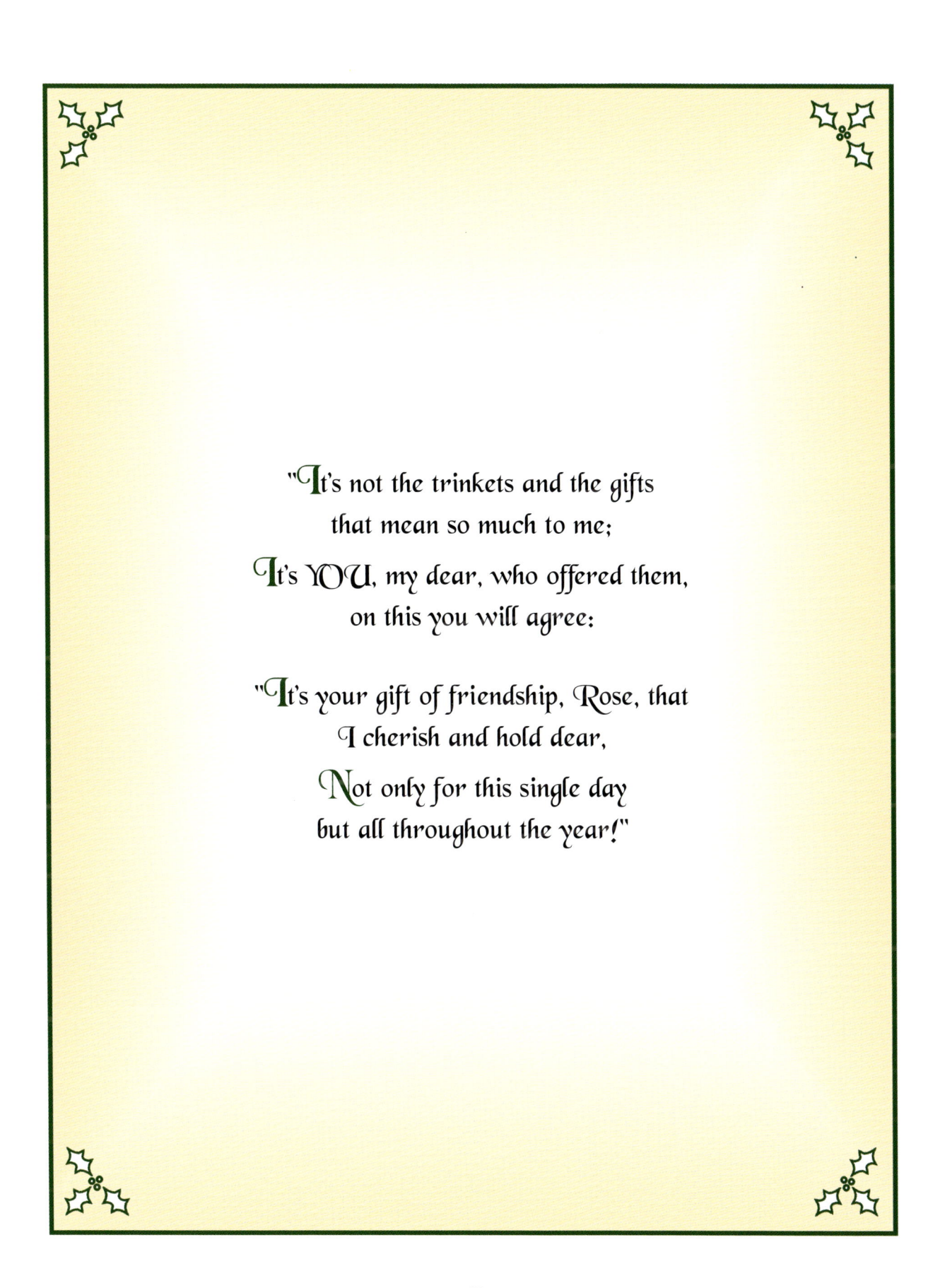

"It's not the trinkets and the gifts
that mean so much to me;

It's YOU, my dear, who offered them,
on this you will agree:

"It's your gift of friendship, Rose, that
I cherish and hold dear,

Not only for this single day
but all throughout the year!"

Grace let go of the trembling hand
to give her gift to Rose,
All wrapped in joyful paper and
tied 'round with little bows.

Rose took the gift and opened it
and saw through anxious eyes,
A book that made her heart well up
that she could not disguise.

Dear friends who love each other
was the topic of the book;
She opened it and turned a page,
just taking a quick look.

"The twilight softly comes to life..."
is what she found inside;

She understood the precious gift
had always been implied.

"Merry Christmas, my dear friend!"
is how the book would end;

Friendship, immortalized in verse,
is given to you, my friend.

Merry Christmas, my dear friend!

"Friendship is the golden ribbon that ties the world together."
- Author Unknown

This book was written to celebrate friendship
as a true gift that can be given
at any time throughout the year.

You may choose to create your own
golden ribbon of friendship by
writing a note and forwarding this book to a friend.

Enjoy your friendships!

Date:
To My Cherished Friend:

Date:
To My Cherished Friend:

Date:
To My Cherished Friend:

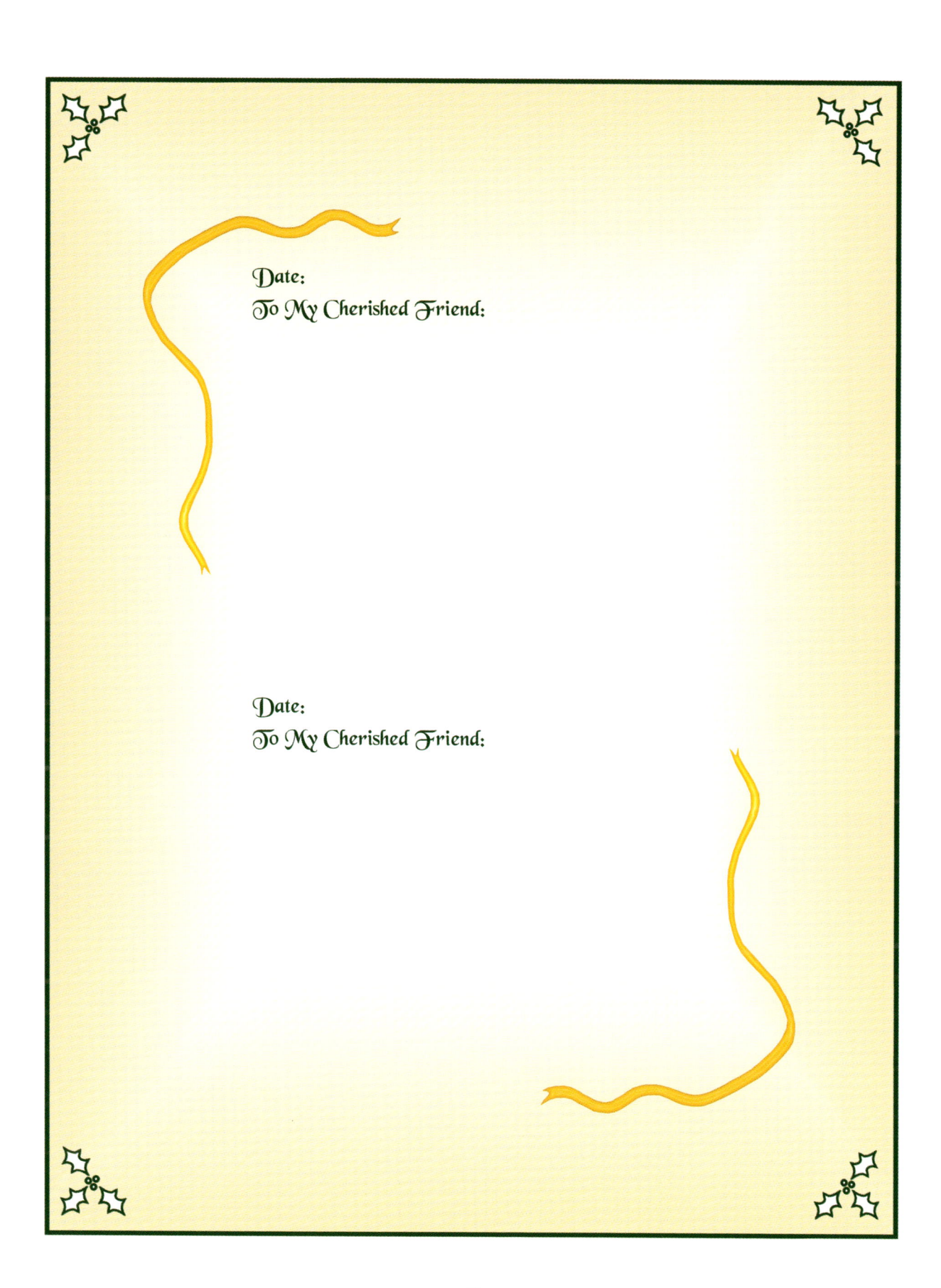

Date:
To My Cherished Friend:

Date:
To My Cherished Friend:

Date:
To My Cherished Friend:

Date:
To My Cherished Friend: